# DATE DUE

| | |
|---|---|
| | |
| | |
| | |
| | |
| | |
| | |
| | |
| | |
| | |
| | |
| | |
| | |
| | |
| | |
| | |

BRODART, CO.                    Cat. No. 23-221

# BE A MAKER

## MAKER PROJECTS FOR KIDS WHO LOVE

# ANI MAT ION

## SARAH LEVETE

## CRABTREE
Publishing Company
www.crabtreebooks.com

# Crabtree Publishing Company

www.crabtreebooks.com

**Author:** Sarah Levete

**Publishing plan research and development:**
Reagan Miller

**Editors:** Sarah Eason, Harriet McGregor,
Reagan Miller

**Proofreaders:** Nancy Dickmann, Janine Deschenes

**Editorial director:** Kathy Middleton

**Design:** Paul Myerscough

**Cover design:** Emma DeBanks

**Photo research:** Rachel Blount

**Production coordinator and**
**Prepress techician:** Tammy McGarr

**Print coordinator:** Margaret Amy Salter

**Consultant:** Chris Stone

Production coordinated by Calcium Creative

**Photo Credits:**

t=Top, bl=Bottom Left, br=Bottom Right

Library of Congress: p. 6; Shutterstock: Complot: p. 4; Jacek
Chabraszewski: p. 26; Extradeda: p. 17; Featureflash: p. 27; Goodluz: p.
24; Paisan Homhuan: p. 8–9; Lapina: pp. 1, 20; Morphart Creation: p. 7;
Olga Phoenix: p. 18; Photo Works: p. 21; Pressmaster: p. 5; Danilo Sanino:
p. 16; Joe Seer: p. 11; Igor Stevanovic: p. 15; Slurpy Studios: p. 25; Studio
AKA: p. 14; David Stringham/Huntington University: pp. 9, 10, 19;
Tudor Photography: pp. 12–13, 22–23, 28–29.

Cover: Tudor Photography.

**Library and Archives Canada Cataloguing in Publication**

Levete, Sarah, author
    Maker projects for kids who love animation / Sarah Levete.

(Be a maker!)
Includes index.
Issued in print and electronic formats.
ISBN 978-0-7787-2244-1 (bound).--
ISBN 978-0-7787-2256-4 (paperback).--
ISBN 978-1-4271-1716-8 (html)

    1. Animation (Cinematography)--Juvenile literature.  I. Title.

TR897.5.L475 2016          j777'.7          C2015-907909-8
                                            C2015-907910-1

**Library of Congress Cataloging-in-Publication Data**

Names: Levete, Sarah, author.
Title: Maker projects for kids who love animation / Sarah Levete.
Description: New York : Crabtree Publishing Company, 2016. |
    Series: Be a  maker! | Includes index. | Description
    based on print version record and CIP data provided by
    publisher; resource not viewed.
Identifiers: LCCN 2015045083 (print) | LCCN 2015042101 (ebook)
    | ISBN 9781427117168 (electronic HTML) | ISBN 9780778722441
    (reinforced library binding : alk. paper) | ISBN 9780778722564
    (pbk. : alk. paper)
Subjects:  LCSH: Animation (Cinematography)--Juvenile
    literature.
Classification: LCC TR897.5 (print) | LCC TR897.5 .L475 2016
    (ebook) | DDC  777/.7--dc23
LC record available at http://lccn.loc.gov/2015045083

## Crabtree Publishing Company

www.crabtreebooks.com          1-800-387-7650

Printed in Canada/022016/MA20151130

**Published in Canada**
**Crabtree Publishing**
616 Welland Ave.
St. Catharines, Ontario
L2M 5V6

**Published in the United States**
**Crabtree Publishing**
PMB 59051
350 Fifth Avenue, 59th Floor
New York, New York 10118

**Published in the United Kingdom**
**Crabtree Publishing**
Maritime House
Basin Road North, Hove
BN41 1WR

**Published in Australia**
**Crabtree Publishing**
3 Charles Street
Coburg North
VIC, 3058

# CONTENTS

# TIME TO MAKE!

Animate anything—literally! To animate something is to bring it to life. Makers can bring nearly anything to life, from drawn images and photographs to clay sculptures and toys. Animation is about experimentation and invention. All you need is imagination and a willingness to try new things. Read on and feel inspired to start your first animation project.

## ILLUSION

Animators create thousands of pictures, known as **frames**, that seem to move when shown in order very quickly. The high speed at which the images are shown tricks the human eye into "seeing" the pictures move. This is an **optical illusion**!

## ANIMATION ALL AROUND

From advertising to movies, animation is all around us. The art of animation is used to entertain, educate, and inform. And it is great fun to create! For example, computer and video games use animation techniques to create characters. Some of today's most popular movies, such as *Inside Out* and *Frozen*, are animated. There are also animations on the Internet that help to clearly explain difficult school subjects, or how to fix things.

Each of these images show a horse jumping and each is slightly different. If they were viewed individually, one after another, the result would be a moving image.

# BEING A MAKER

The maker philosophy is about working on projects and exploring possibilities. It is about **innovation**, learning from things that do not go quite according to plan, and not giving up. Collaboration, or working with others as a team, is a key part of the maker movement. Even if you do not work on your animation projects with other makers, sharing ideas, offering and asking for feedback, and celebrating each other's work will help you succeed.

## MAKERSPACES

**Makerspaces** are places in your community where like-minded people can go to share knowledge and resources, be inspired, and to bring their projects to life. Other makers will be excited to hear about, and help you with, your animation projects, and you can get involved in their projects, too. Makerspaces can be found in places like community centers and libraries.

## GET STARTED

Start animating with simple projects, and then make them as complex as you want. Adapt the suggested projects to suit your ideas. Let your creativity flow and see where it takes you. Be inspired by the history of animation and see how people have crafted success from the challenges and opportunities of this art form.

Get together with others to share ideas. Together you may come up with ideas about animating all kinds of objects.

# ALL ABOUT ANIMATION

The idea of animation has existed for centuries, but the techniques used to animate have changed and **evolved**. Animation is a constantly developing art form. This makes it perfect for makers who are interested in new challenges, developing ideas, and just giving it a shot.

## EARLY DEVICES

One of the first known devices, or pieces of equipment, used to create a sense of movement from still images was the "Magic Lantern." It is not clear who first invented it, but this device was used by a German scholar, Athanasius Kircher, in 1640. He drew several images on glass slides and then inserted these into the Magic Lantern. He moved the glass slides with string and when the drawings were projected onto a wall, they gave the illusion of movement.

This engraving from the eighteenth century shows people looking at ghostly illusions created by a Magic Lantern. They are shocked because the illusions look as though they are real.

# ANIMATION IN TOYS

Fast-forward to the nineteenth century, when inventors and scientists began to experiment with ways to make pictures "move." These inventions were often toys. The zoetrope was a popular toy in the nineteenth century. It was shaped like a drum with an opening at the top. Inside were hand-drawn images. When the child spun the drum around and looked through the slots on the outside, the images appeared to move.

# EDISON'S KINETOSCOPE

Thomas Alva Edison invented the kinetoscope in 1891, a box through which a reel of photos was passed at 46 frames a minute. Edison asked New York newspaper cartoonist James Stuart Blackton to do a series of drawings. Edison took photographs of them. Edison worked with Blackton to release the cartoonist's 3,000 drawings as a **sequence** in motion. It was called *Humorous Phases of Funny Faces*. Animation was on the move.

This is a sketch of a zoetrope. Inside the toy are images of a running horse. As the toy spins, the horse seems to move.

## Be a Maker!

Animation is about putting together images so that they appear to move. There are many types of animation, created using different techniques. Some are created on a computer, others created using paper, and some are created by using three-dimensional (3-D) **models.** Whatever the technique used, the effect is to create a sense of movement from still images.

# ANIMATION TECHNIQUES

Early animated films were created by taking photographs of hundreds of drawings to create a moving image. Today's animation is often made on a computer, using sophisticated programs to create realistic and detailed sequences.

## TRADITIONAL ANIMATION

Hand-drawn images were used for early movies, such as the Mickey Mouse **cartoons**. Animators used pencil and paper, and had to redraw every single image, each with a small difference. Later, figures were drawn on layers of transparent celluloid sheets, or **cels**. A cel was placed on top of the drawn background so the animator did not have to redraw the background for every frame. This transformed the speed of the process and the accuracy of the drawing.

# Be a Maker!

Early animators lost a lot of work if they later discovered they had made an error. They had no way of checking their work and correcting it as they went along. Today's animators and makers also need to be resilient and patient. Have you ever been in a situation where you have worked on a drawing or project only to discover that it is not quite right? How do you deal with that? What are effective ways to cope when a project does not go as planned?

# STOP-MOTION ANIMATION

This type of animation uses objects such as toys or models instead of drawings. The animator changes the object's position or pose for each frame to create a sense of movement when the frames are shown in rapid succession.

# COMPUTER ANIMATION

With computer animation, a computer program is used to design and draw the scenes and images, and even create 3-D images. Putting the sequence of images together is also done on a computer—no cameras needed! *Toy Story* was the first full-length computer-generated (CG) movie, in 1995.

WALL-E starred in the computer-animated movie of the same name. You can use similar toys to create your own stop-motion animations.

With computer animation, images can be incredibly detailed. They can even appear to be 3-D.

# MOVIE ANIMATION

Animation has never stood still, thanks to the makers and innovators who have found new ways to ensure it continues to evolve. Some movie animation today shows characters and scenes in extraordinary detail. The movie-making process involves hundreds of people.

## TEAMWORK AND COLLABORATION

Animators often work in teams and collaborate with other animators or makers. Even though it was Walt Disney who first sketched Mickey Mouse, another Disney animator, Ub Iwerks, created the final design for Mickey. In those early days of movie animation, animators completed all the drawings. Over time, it became obvious that the animators could not draw quickly enough. People called "in-betweeners" were employed to draw the pictures in between the key images.

Teamwork was key for the "49 Hour Film Competition." Five teams had only 49 hours to produce an animated movie.

# Makers and Shakers

## Walt Disney

Walt Disney (1901–1966) gave his name to one of the world's most influential animation studios. However, the studio did experience some difficulties during the early years. The first company he set up with Ub Iwerks failed when it did not make enough money. However, Walt had resilience and determination, just like any good maker. When he had the idea for a full-length color animated movie retelling the story of *Snow White and the Seven Dwarfs*, people said it would be a terrible failure. Released in 1937, it was a huge success.

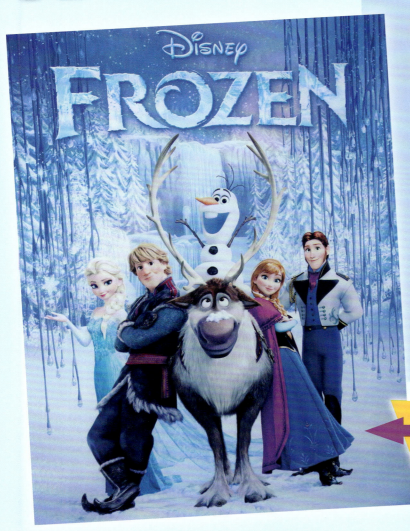

## LONG AND DETAILED

Today's **blockbuster** animations take years to complete. In Disney's *Frozen* (2013), there is a famous scene in which the character Elsa conjures up a palace from snowflakes. Animating this scene required the skills of more than 50 people working for nine months. It took 4,000 computers more than 30 hours to **render** each frame for the sequence. In the finished movie, the sequence lasts just 36 seconds!

The animators of *Frozen* used special software to create up to 2,000 different snowflakes in the movie.

11

# MAKE IT!
# CREATE A FLIP-BOOK

Forget high-tech gizmos—start your animation with this simple but hugely effective **flip-book**. It demonstrates the principles of animation and gives you instant results using just paper and a pen. A flip-book presents a series of pictures in rapid succession so that when you flip through it, you "see" a moving image. For best results, choose a simple "action" to draw, like a ball bouncing.

## YOU WILL NEED

- Sticky notepad (or make a pad using small sheets of thin paper, held together along one edge using staples)
- Dark ballpoint pen

**1**

- Start on the last sheet of the pad and work backward. Test the technique by drawing a round shape on the last note or page.
- Put the next piece of paper over the top of the one you have drawn on. You should be able to see through the paper to your original drawing.
- Draw a round shape slightly lower than the original.
- Continue this for about 20 pages.
- Flip through the pages, starting at the back. The shape seems to move.

## 2

- Follow the same principle as in step 1, but this time draw your own image.
- Continue to draw the same image on each piece of paper, introducing a small change each time. For example, if you choose to draw an animal jumping, change the angle of the back legs slightly in your second drawing. The legs will straighten as the animal jumps up.
- Continue to draw on a new piece of paper until you reach your final image.

## 3

- Time to flip! At a regular pace, flip the pages. You will see your drawing come to life!

## CONCLUSION

Show a friend your flip-book. Ask him or her for their views.

- What makes it work, and what could be done better? Flick through the flip-book yourself with a critical eye.
- Do you agree with your friend, or are there other ways you can improve your first animation?

## Make It Even Better!

Experiment with a different action by adding additional detail—maybe try out a stick person performing cartwheels. This may need some additional pages to make it effective.

# SCRIPT TO SCREEN

You have already discovered that animation can be applied to a simple idea, such as making a stick figure run, or an incredibly complex and sophisticated story that takes years to complete. Whether it is a **short** or longer movie, makers spend a lot of time thinking and planning before actually filming.

## PURPOSE OF A STORYBOARD

A **storyboard** involves drawing and writing down the key ideas of an animation so that the actual process of animation, whether by hand or on computer, is effective and efficient. The storyboard is made up of panels. Each panel represents a frame. The animator adds notes, such as a summary of the mood of the frame. For example, the animator says whether it is a happy, sad, or scary scene. Sound effects or recorded dialogue can be added to an animation and these can be detailed in the storyboard. Each panel maps the changes that take place.

In movies, studios employ storyboard artists. Their job is to illustrate the story, plan shots, and show the action of the animation.

The storyboard brings together ideas from many makers, because it reflects mood, background, music, and story.

# USING YOUR STORYBOARD

As you become more advanced in your animation, you can add notes about how you want the movie to look. Draw the first three or four key scenes of your storyboard. Add information such as whether there is going to be any sound or if the scene is going to be brightly lit or dark. Make sure that the scenes tell the story in your mind. Next, find the objects you need for your movie.

A storyboard shows what will happen in each key frame of your animation.

## Be a Maker!

Animating is an evolving process. You may need to make a lot of changes to your storyboard as you go. Flexibility and openness to new ideas is crucial for a maker, and for the success of your movie. Ideas grow and change. When you start your storyboard, how prepared are you to make changes if the ideas do not work out? What benefits can you see from being able to adapt the storyboard?

# STOP! MOTION

Stop-motion is a popular and accessible way for makers to animate. Drawing skills are not necessary! All the maker needs is an object to animate, a story, a **digital camera**, and a computer equipped with a basic video editing program.

## GRADUAL CHANGE

Makers need a lot of patience and a good sense of humor to create stop-motion animation, because it is a time-consuming art. It takes about 12 frames (shots) per second to smoothly show an audience a smile turning into a scowl. Tim Burton's movie *The Nightmare Before Christmas* (1993) used 227 puppets, one of which had 400 different heads to show changing moods and emotions. It took three years for a crew of 100 to complete the movie!

## TAKING SHOTS

With a digital camera (or webcam), the animator takes a photograph of the object, moves the object very slightly, and takes another photograph. This continues until the action or move is complete.

Each of these frames shows a snapshot of a chimp walking. In a movie, you would see all of the frames in series in little more than one second.

The animator can download the still images to a computer and then **edit** the sequence using video editing software. There are a number of good, free software packages available that can do this type of work, such as Blender. The animator can then add music or sound effects.

Before you film your stop-motion project, take a look around for materials that you can use. Think outside the box—what can you bring to life, and how? What story are you going to tell? How are you going to show changes in the characters?

This character is made from junk. Animation became "junkmation" in making *The Legend of the Sky Kingdom* (see below).

## Makers and Shakers

### Roger Hawkins

In 2004, a team of 14 moviemakers from Zimbabwe made an animated movie by recycling discarded junk. The models animated in the movie, *The Legend of the Sky Kingdom*, were made from old upcycled car parts and tools. Money to fund the movie came partly from the sale of eggs from the producer's poultry business. The animation was a hit at the International Animated Film Festival. Director Roger Hawkins said, "We are amazed that, as a few people who dared to dream and had the courage and foolishness to try something, people around the world can be touched by what we have done." Now, that is a maker!

# SETTING UP FOR ACTION

Whatever method a maker is going to use to create a project, he or she needs to consider:

- Who is the subject of the movie?
- Where will it be set?
- What will happen?

You can use your own models, or items such as toys. You might want to mix it up a little, if that suits your story.

## SHARING IDEAS

Once you have created your storyboard, added notes, and found the objects you need for your scenes, ask whether any of your friends would like to team up to discuss making the movie. Sharing your ideas helps find solutions to difficulties, and working in a team increases the talent available. Someone may be more confident using a camera and another person may excel at drawing.

## Be a Maker!

**What do you do when things do not go to plan? According to Ed Catmull, head of top animation studio Pixar, failing is an important part of success.**

**"A lot of things we learn in life are from our failures," Catmull said. "Solving the problems we face is not an impediment to the job: it is the job. Ease is not the goal, excellence is."**

**When you start an animation or another project, what is your approach when it does not work?**

# PRACTICALITIES

A kitchen table is great for filming, but if you are creating an animated scene using models and objects, the scene may need to stay in the same place for a while. You may need a table that will not be used regularly for other purposes. Filming on a sunny day provides great light, but weather conditions vary and the change in light will be reflected in your final movie. A couple of lamps pointed toward your scene are all you need to provide constant light levels.

# RESEARCH

Animators on *Frozen* worked in sunny southern California. Their film was set in snowy Norway, in Europe. The team went on a snowy field trip to experience the feel of snow. They each trudged through the snow in a ball gown (like the heroine in the movie) to find out what if felt like so they could recreate the detail in their drawings. Most animators do not go to such lengths, but it is important to have an understanding of what you are animating.

Before you start, set everything in place, from models to lights. Then you can focus on the animation.

# STOP-MOTION MATERIALS

The beauty of stop-motion animation is that you can animate anything as long as you can move it easily. Clay, which is soft and flexible, has given a new twist to animation. It has even created a new term—Claymation. Clay and similar materials can be handled and moved while keeping their shape. Just add your imagination!

Modeling clay is an ideal material for stop-motion—it is flexible but firm, easy to work with, and comes in a variety of colors for added interest.

## CLAYMATION

Some Claymation models have a skeleton structure to help the model move. This is called an **armature**, and it is usually made from wire or steel. The skeleton is covered with clay. The armature supports the weight of the clay, so the animators can move the pieces of the model without it losing its shape or rigidity. Making an armature can be as simple or as complex as you need. A frame can be as simple as a strong, flexible wire, while more detailed frames involve sockets and joints.

## SKETCHING

Before you start making your model, draw some sketches—they can be really rough. Think about what you need your model to do. This will influence how you make your model. Link this development work to your storyboard. The whole begins to come together.

# MATERIAL VARIETY

There are plenty of other materials to use besides clay. From cardboard to yarn, any shape or texture will work. **Cutout** paper characters work well to create simple but effective images. A paper character is cut into different parts, which are joined with something like poster putty so that the animator can easily move them. Features such as a raised eyebrow can easily be taped onto the character to show motion.

**Shadow puppets** have movable parts. These can be laid flat, back-lit, and animated.

## Makers and Shakers

### Lotte Reiniger

As a schoolgirl, Lotte Reiniger (1899–1981), was fascinated by shadow puppets, the **traditional** Indonesian method of storytelling. She presented many shadow puppet shows to her friends. Soon, she became interested in movies and, through determination and hard work, she combined her two passions. Lotte made a 66-minute movie called *The Adventures of Prince Achmed* (1926). She cut out and photographed 24 pictures for each second of film—that is about 100,000 cutout silhouettes. Lotte said, "My hands have been using scissors for so long now that they know for themselves what they have to do."

21

# MAKE IT!
# MAKE A MODEL

Making a model for stop-motion is fun, but needs thought. Remember, your model is going to animate your story. Think about your story and keep it simple. You can use this project as a starting point for developing a larger or more ambitious project later. After all, the character "Gromit" from Aardman Studios' *A Grand Day Out* (1989) was first sketched as a cat before making it to the big screen as a dog!

## YOU WILL NEED
- Material for your model, such as soft modeling clay. It needs to be flexible, but firm enough to hold a shape
- Flat board on which to make your model
- Toothpicks
- Any extra items your model will need, such as, pens, buttons, beads, or pipe cleaners
- Camera

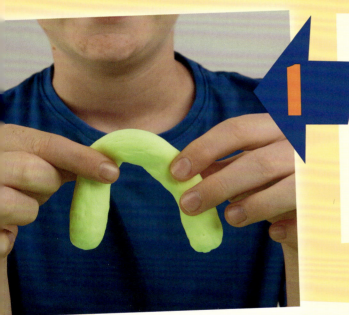

**1**
- Play around with the material you have chosen. Roll it, pull it, stretch it, and twist it.
- How does it hold its shape?
- Will it stand unsupported?

**2**
- Put your model together. Keep it a manageable size. Too small, and it will be difficult to pick up detail when you film. Too large, and it might not fit in the frame.
- Make sure that important body parts are easy to see. Remember, if you need to move a part of a model many times (to show movement from one pose to another), the part must be strong enough not to break.

**3**

- Add on any design features, such as eyes, expressions, or props. Use whatever you have at hand. Be resourceful!

**4**

- With a digital camera, tablet, or webcam, take stills of each frame, or movement. Try it out at first with a small movement.
- Play it back through computer software such as iMovies or Windows Movie Maker. Make any adjustments, and then film your original idea.
- Do you need to rethink any aspects?

## Make It Even Better!

**Reflect on ways to improve and add to your model. It might be useful to create another model made from similar material, or even from upcycled materials or old toys. You have worked with a 3-D model (a model that has depth). Can you try a cutout—a flat** two-dimensional (2-D) **image? Maybe it will help to use some kind of mount for your tablet or a tripod for your camera. This will make sure the photograph is taken from exactly the same spot each time.**

## CONCLUSION

When you have watched the finished animation, think about what works and what does not. Does the model express what you wanted to show in the animation? How would you change it? Think about the robustness of the model—it may need more work to feature in a longer project.

# CHANGING TIMES

Animation has been transformed by technological developments. Computer software allows animators working with traditional hand drawings to **upload** photographs of the drawings to a program that will show the animation. Other software allows animators to create scenes of amazing complexity.

## FREE!

Some animation software can be freely downloaded from the Internet. Your computer may contain built-in video editing software. If you are using a digital camera, upload photographs of your hand drawings or models to a computer and use software to string the images together.

## HAIR-RAISING

More advanced software helps create a more realistic look, but it can introduce other problems. Action hero Merida in the animated movie *Brave* (2012) has thick, wild, and curly hair, which bounces around with every move she makes. When the animation team were told what Merida's hair was going to look like, they were worried that they would not be able to get it right. It took six research engineers and artists more than three and a half years to bring the flaming red head of hair to the big screen.

Merida's brilliant red hair helps to create a vibrant, heroic character on screen, but involved hours of painstaking research and work.

24

# TRADITIONAL AND TECHNOLOGICAL

A five-minute animated short called *Paperman* (2012) was created with new software. It allowed animators to hand-draw on a tablet. It is an incredibly complex piece of software, but it enabled the skills of traditional animation to merge with the advances of technology.

Some computer software allows you to design and create all of your work on a computer.

## Makers and Shakers

### Adamu Waziri

Nigerian animator Adamu Waziri wanted children in Africa to see cartoons that reflected their lives. Because few were available, he created his own. His educational cartoon, *Bino and Fino*, is made from cutouts. A team of seven people now work on *Bino and Fino*, which is shown in several African countries and around the world. It is the first ever children's educational cartoon produced in Nigeria.

# WORLD OF ANIMATION

The step-by-step process of creating an animation encourages the maker to think critically about the action or activity he or she is creating in the animation. Thinking about and breaking down an activity or scene can help make complex ideas seem simpler.

## ATOMIC ANIMATION

Atoms are the microscopic particles that make up everything in the universe. But what does an atom have to do with animation? Researchers at an international company were investigating the use of atoms for data storage. They decided to share their passion and enthusiasm. They used a special microscope to magnify the appearance of atoms 100 million times. The environment had to be kept very cold at –436° Fahrenheit (–260° C) to keep the atoms still. Slowly and carefully, the team moved the position of each atom, frame by frame, to create a moving stick figure. The result is the world's tiniest movie, titled
*A Boy and His Atom* (2013).

Enjoy the process of making your models or putting together a cutout. Use the animation to tell a story or to illustrate an idea.

# MADE TO SHARE

It has never been easier to share your work and ideas. Animators often start out by uploading their projects to websites such as YouTube. It is a good way to get your work seen, but be sure to ask permission from an adult first. A Maker Faire is another great place to share ideas with others. These are events where you can submit your maker projects and celebrate science, arts, crafts, engineering, and the maker can-do attitude.

Go online to check out what other makers have been up to. Maker sites reveal an amazing array of talent and ideas. From animated **pizzoetropes** to felt puppets fighting, animation is there for the making. If you can, visit a local makerspace and get involved. Who knows what you will create?

Nick Park (left) and Steve Box, creators of Wallace and Gromit, received awards for their work.

## Be a Maker!

**Can you think of ways that you could use animation to help explain a process? When you are asked to prepare a presentation, you might think about using a slideshow document on the computer or making a poster. What about animating your project? There is no better way to begin to understand a process. Perhaps join forces with a group of classmates to work on something together.**

# MAKE IT!
# SHOW TIME!

Bring together your ideas and enthusiasm! Get together with a group of friends to complete an animation with a background, sound, and strong story. Start with your storyboard and figure out exactly what you are going to animate. Think about everyone's role in the project and be sure to draw on your friends' interests and skills.

**1**

- Create a background. Upcycle materials wherever possible. You might find these around your home, in a thrift store, or out in the natural world. Remember that all of the objects must be sized so that they will fit in the frame. The objects must also be strong enough to withstand repeated movement.

**2**

- Position your models or objects on the background and take a photograph.
- Move the objects slightly for each frame so that they are telling your story.
- Upload the photos to your computer.

- Record any sound effects and dialogue onto your phone, tablet, or computer, or download sound effects from the Internet. You must check whether you need legal permission to use prerecorded music.
- Edit the movie so that your frames appear in the right order, and that sound effects and dialogue are introduced at the right times.

**3**

**4**

- Invite friends and family to watch the show.

## CONCLUSION

Give yourself a round of applause for completing your first filmed animation! When you watch it, relax and enjoy it. How would the animation change if you used a different technique, such as drawing? Would you use a mount to hold the camera in one position?

## Make It Even Better!

**Could you develop your idea into a longer animation, or could you focus on one part of the animation to develop it in a new way? Keep trying new ideas and enjoy your animation!**

# GLOSSARY

**armature** A framework on which a model is built

**blockbuster** Something that is very successful

**cartoons** Movies made using animation techniques or simple drawings showing characters' features in an exaggerated way

**cels** Short for celluloids: the transparent sheets on which animation drawings are traced and colored

**cutout** A flat animation figure with moveable parts, cut from paper or another material

**digital camera** A camera that records information as digital data instead of on film

**edit** To cut and move around to improve your animation

**evolved** Changed and developed

**flip-book** A book with images that seem to move as the pages are flipped

**frames** Individual shots

**innovation** The creation of something new, such as a new idea, method, or device

**makerspaces** Places where makers gather to innovate, share resources, and learn from one another

**optical illusion** A trick of the eye

**pizzoetropes** Turntables that spin a pizza. Toppings are used to create an animation as the pizza spins

**render** To use powerful computers to build all the digital information into a single frame of film

**resilient** Able to move on from difficulties and challenges

**sequence** Two or more actions that take place in order

**shadow puppets** Flat cutout puppets shown behind a screen as shadows

**short** A short movie

**storyboard** A way to visually map ideas

**three-dimensional (3-D)** An image that has height, width, and gives the impression of depth

**traditonal** Something that has been done for a long period of time

**two-dimensional (2-D)** An image that has height and width but no depth

**upload** To transfer data from one device to another

# LEARNING MORE

## BOOKS

Cassidy, John, and Nicholas Berger. *The Klutz Book of Animation: Make Your Own Stop Motion Movies*. Klutz, 2010.

Eckerson, Nate. *Stopmotion Explosion: Animate Anything and Make Movies—Epic Films for $20 or Less*. Stopmotion Explosion, 2011.

Murphy, Mary. *Beginner's Guide to Animation: Everything You Need to Know to Get Started*. Watson Guptil, 2008.

Piercy, Helen. *Animation Studio*. Candlewick Press, 2013.

## WEBSITES

For a wide variety of projects at all levels, from stop-motion and computer generated imagery, to background design and character development, visit:
**diy.org/skills/animator**

This online maker magazine is full of maker ideas and links, including examples of animation and suggestions for free software:
**www.makezine.com**

Discover some great examples of different types of flip-book animation to inspire you at:
**www.nyfa.edu/student-resources/flipbook-animation-techniques-and-examples**

For all you need to know about stop motion animation, including demonstrations of Claymation and "how to" guides, to upload your own animations, and to get advice on your projects, visit:
**www.stopmotioncentral.com**

# INDEX